ANIMAL ATTACK!

Hunting with GREAT WHITE SHARKS

WITHDRAWN

By Hunter Reynolds

Gareth Stevens
Publishing

Please visit our website, www.garethstevens.com. For a free color catalog of all our high-quality books, call toll free 1-800-542-2595 or fax 1-877-542-2596.

Library of Congress Cataloging-in-Publication Data

Reynolds, Hunter.
 Hunting with great white sharks / Hunter Reynolds.
  p. cm. — (Animal attack!)
 Includes index.
 ISBN 978-1-4339-7076-4 (pbk.)
 ISBN 978-1-4339-7077-1 (6-pack)
 ISBN 978-1-4339-7075-7 (library binding)
 1. White shark—Juvenile literature. I. Title.
 QL638.95.L3R49 2013
 597.3'3—dc23

2012008130

First Edition

Published in 2013 by
Gareth Stevens Publishing
111 East 14th Street, Suite 349
New York, NY 10003

Copyright © 2013 Gareth Stevens Publishing

Designer: Katelyn E. Reynolds
Editor: Greg Roza

Photo credits: Cover, p. 1, (cover, pp. 1, 3–24 background image) PM Images/Photodisc/Getty Images; cover, pp. 1, 3–24 (background graphic) pashabo/Shutterstock.com; cover, pp. 4–23 (splatter graphic) jgl247/Shutterstock.com; p. 5 Stephen Frink/Photographer's Choice/Getty Images; p. 6 Vlad61/Shutterstock.com; p. 7 frantisekhojdysz/Shutterstock.com; pp. 9, 17 Fuse/Getty Images; p. 10 Chris Harvey/Shutterstock.com; p. 11 Natursports/Shutterstock.com; pp. 12–13 kbrowne41/Shutterstock.com; p. 14 Dave King/Dorling Kindersley/Getty Images; p. 15 David Fleetham/Visuals Unlimited, Inc./Getty Images; p. 18 Daniel M. Silva/Shutterstock.com; p. 19 Jeff Rotman/The Image Bank/Getty Images; p. 20 Jeffrey L. Rotman/Peter Arnold/Getty Images.

Printed in the United States of America

CPSIA compliance information: Batch #CS12GS: For further information contact Gareth Stevens, New York, New York at 1-800-542-2595.

CONTENTS

Words in the glossary appear in **bold** type
the first time they are used in the text.

DEADLY PREDATOR

The great white shark is one of the planet's deadliest **predators**. It has powerful jaws and thousands of sharp teeth. It's also a super swimmer with strong senses.

Thanks to movies and stories, the great white shark has long been known as a man-eater. However, as you'll soon learn, this isn't completely true. While shark attacks on people do happen, sharks mostly prefer to hunt animals that live in or near the ocean.

Fact Hunter

Sharks have been in Earth's oceans for about 400 million years.

Great whites may not be the man-eaters that many people think they are, but you wouldn't want to be this close to one.

▽

WHERE TO FIND GREAT WHITES

Great white sharks can be found in **temperate** seas throughout the world. They're often found in colder waters as well. They've been spotted off the coasts of Canada and Alaska.

Great whites spend most of their time close to shore. They can also be found near **reefs** and islands where their favorite foods dwell. However, they can be found out at sea as well, and they may dive more than 820 feet (250 m) beneath the water's surface.

Unlike most other sharks and fish, great whites are **warm-blooded**. That means they can swim in colder waters. It also means they need to eat more.

Great whites prefer cooler waters because warmer waters cause their bodies to overheat.

Great white sharks can grow to about 20 feet (6 m) long. Instead of bone, their **skeleton** is made of a light, bendable matter called cartilage. We have cartilage in our noses and ears. Cartilage allows sharks to swim faster.

The "white" in the great white's name comes from the color of its belly. This makes it hard for **prey** swimming below a great white to see it. However, the rest of the shark is gray. This makes it hard for prey swimming above a shark to see it.

Fact Hunter

The great white's body is narrow on each end and wider in the middle. This shape is called fusiform, and it helps the shark zip quickly through the water.

Most adult great whites are between 13 and 16 feet (4 and 4.9 m) long and weigh between about 1,500 and 2,450 pounds (680 and 1,100 kg).

9

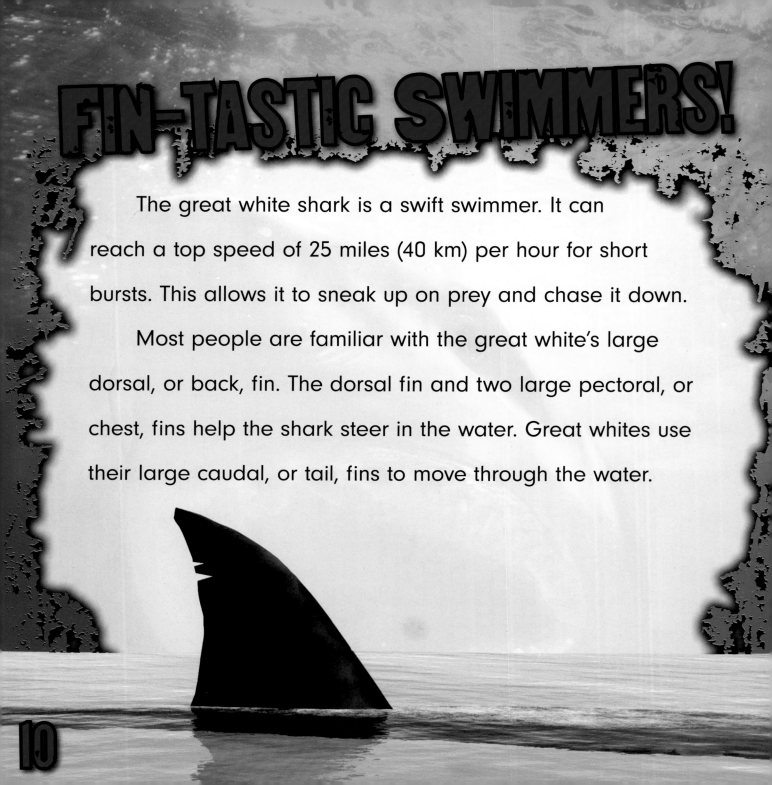

FIN-TASTIC SWIMMERS!

The great white shark is a swift swimmer. It can reach a top speed of 25 miles (40 km) per hour for short bursts. This allows it to sneak up on prey and chase it down.

Most people are familiar with the great white's large dorsal, or back, fin. The dorsal fin and two large pectoral, or chest, fins help the shark steer in the water. Great whites use their large caudal, or tail, fins to move through the water.

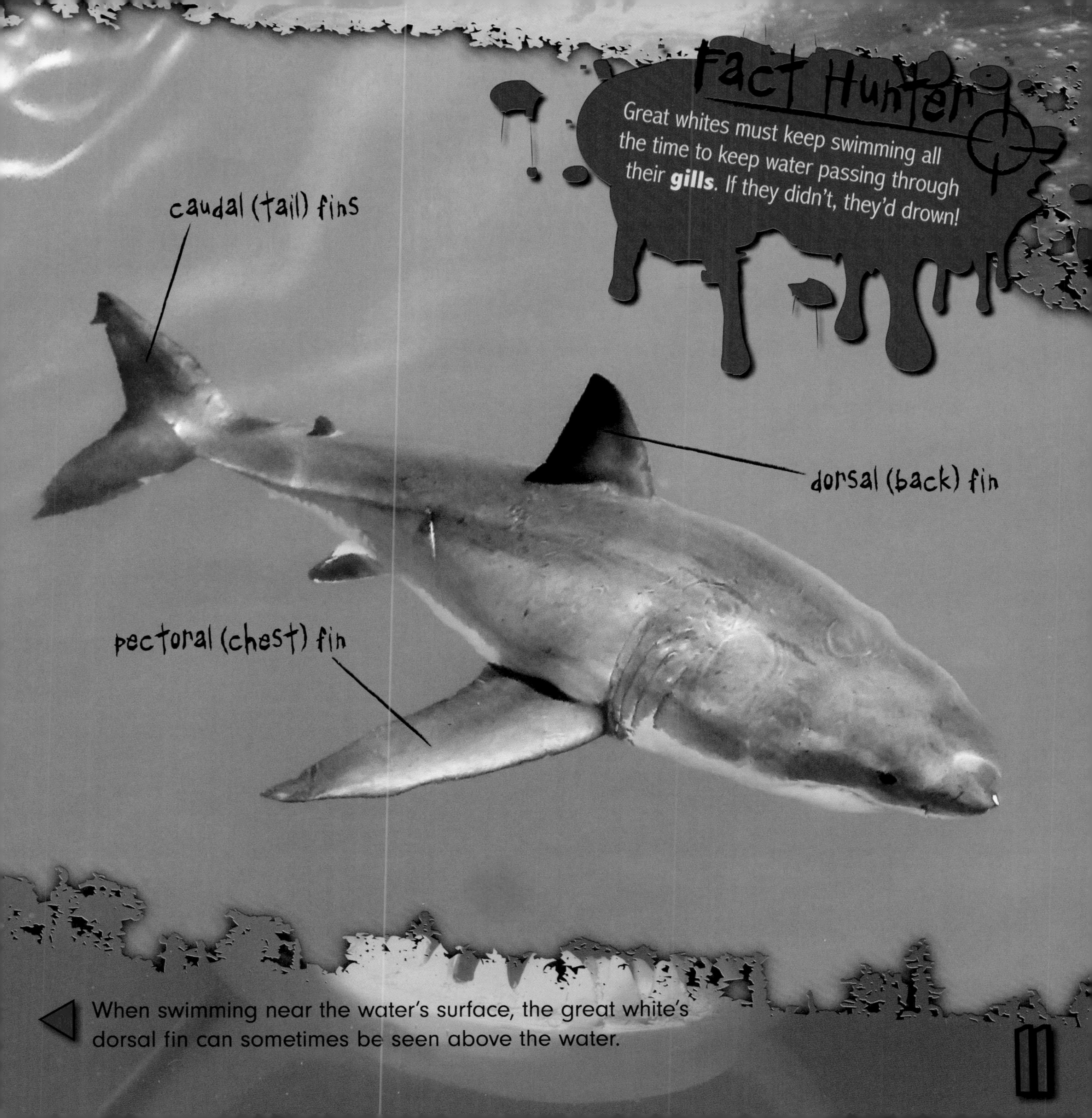

caudal (tail) fins

Fact Hunter

Great whites must keep swimming all the time to keep water passing through their **gills**. If they didn't, they'd drown!

dorsal (back) fin

pectoral (chest) fin

When swimming near the water's surface, the great white's dorsal fin can sometimes be seen above the water.

SHARK SENSES

Over the course of millions of years, great white sharks have **evolved** amazing senses, making them deadly hunters. Their strongest sense is smell. Great whites can smell a drop of blood in 25 gallons (95 l) of water. They can also smell tiny amounts of blood up to 3 miles (4.8 km) away.

Great whites see and hear very well, too. Their eyes have two parts. One sees well during the day, and the other sees well at night.

Fact Hunter

Great white sharks have taste buds just like we do.

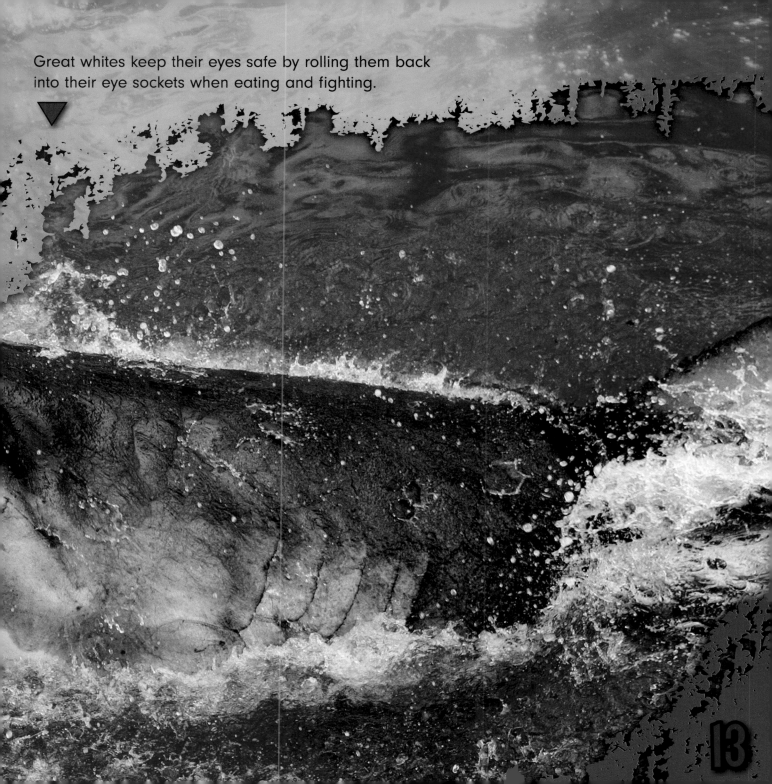

Great whites keep their eyes safe by rolling them back into their eye sockets when eating and fighting.

▽

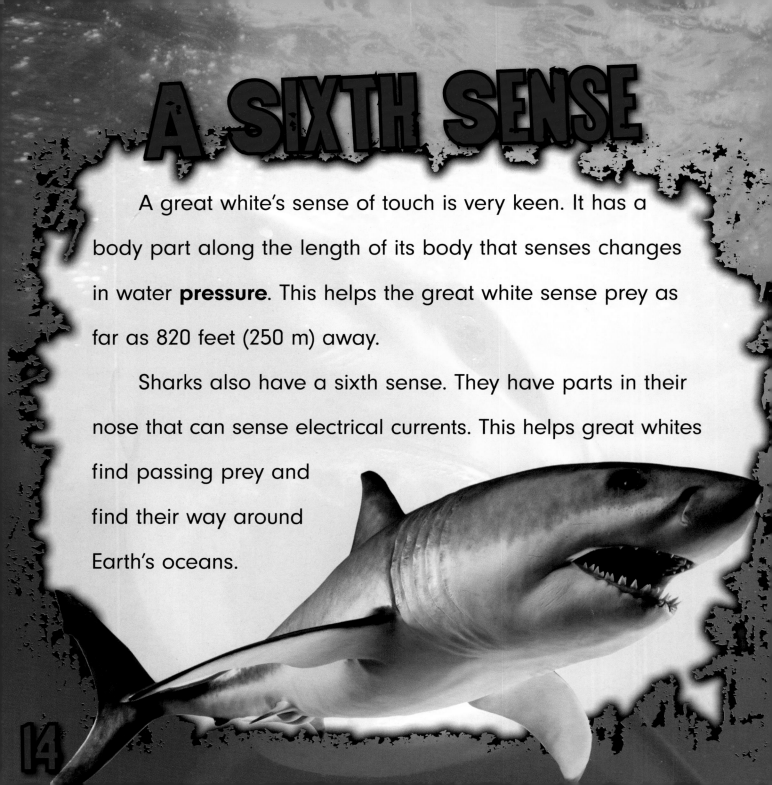

A SIXTH SENSE

A great white's sense of touch is very keen. It has a body part along the length of its body that senses changes in water **pressure**. This helps the great white sense prey as far as 820 feet (250 m) away.

Sharks also have a sixth sense. They have parts in their nose that can sense electrical currents. This helps great whites find passing prey and find their way around Earth's oceans.

14

The great white shark's electricity-sensing body parts are called the ampullae (am-PU-lee) of Lorenzini. Other fish, such as rays and sturgeons, have them, too.

The dark spots on this great white's snout are holes containing the ampullae of Lorenzini.

15

DEADLY SMILE

An adult great white has about 3,000 sharp, pointed teeth. These teeth are serrated. This means they have jagged edges like a saw. When a great white bites down on prey, its top and bottom teeth fit together and "saw" the prey to pieces. Then the shark swallows the pieces whole.

Great whites are always losing teeth. In fact, a single shark may lose and replace 30,000 teeth during its life!

Fact Hunter

Great whites belong to the scientific group Carcharodon (kahr-KEHR-uh-don). This word comes from the Greek words for "ragged" and "tooth."

Inside the mouth of a great white are three rows of teeth. When a shark loses a tooth in front, another moves forward to take its place.

WHO'S HUNGRY?

Great whites eat fish, seals, sea lions, porpoises, and even dead whales. They prefer fatty meals, especially seals with a lot of **blubber**.

Great whites usually approach prey silently from below. They're known to "test taste" prey by giving it a single bite. If the shark likes the taste, it comes back to finish the job. The first bite also causes the prey to bleed and lose strength. Sometimes sharks wait for the animal to die before coming back.

Great white sharks will eat seabirds that land on the water's surface to rest.

19

Great white sharks have just one enemy—people.

Sport fishers consider the great white a challenge to catch.

Many great whites are injured or killed by commercial fishing

lines and nets. Some countries catch great

whites just for their fins, which are used to

make soup.

Many people around the world are

working to reduce the number of great

whites killed by human activities. Even

these deadly hunters need our help to survive.

20

Facts About Great Whites

- Great white sharks have been known to go a month and a half without eating.

- Great whites are speedy biters. It takes a great white just one second to open its mouth and close it again on a meal.

- A great white's bite is nearly twice as strong as a lion's bite.

- Shark cartilage breaks down completely in salt water. That's why complete shark **fossils** are rare.

- Unlike complete shark fossils, shark teeth fossils are plentiful. They're made of matter harder than cartilage.

- In 2004, scientists tracked a great white shark that swam from South Africa to western Australia and back. The trip of 6,800 miles (10,940 km) took just 9 months.

- It's very difficult to keep great whites alive in an aquarium. The longest a great white has lived in **captivity** is 198 days.

GLOSSARY

blubber: a thick layer of fat

captivity: the state of being caged

evolve: to grow and change over time

fossil: the remains or marks of plants or animals that lived thousands or millions of years ago

gill: the body part that ocean animals such as fish use to breathe in water

predator: an animal that hunts other animals for food

pressure: a force that pushes on something else

prey: an animal that is hunted by other animals for food

reef: a chain of rocks or coral, or a ridge of sand, at or near the water's surface

skeleton: the strong frame that supports an animal's body

temperate: mild climate that is never too hot or too cold

warm-blooded: having a body temperature that remains the same, despite the temperature of the surroundings

FOR MORE INFORMATION

Books

Mathea, Heidi. *Great White Sharks*. Edina, MN: ABDO, 2011.

Owings, Lisa. *The Great White Shark*. Minneapolis, MN: Bellwether Media, 2012.

Randolph, Joanne. *The Great White Shark: King of the Ocean*. New York, NY: PowerKids Press, 2007.

Websites

Amazing Animals: Great White Shark Quiz
animals.howstuffworks.com/fish/great-white-shark-quiz.htm
See photographs and take a quiz about great white sharks.

Great White Sharks
kids.nationalgeographic.com/kids/animals/creaturefeature/great-white-shark/
Read more about great whites and see amazing photographs.

INDEX